MW01180930

The Best Investment Money Can't Buy

This Book Will Change Your Life

Eric England

The Best Investment Money Can't Buy

To: _____

From: _____

This is the best gift I can ever give to you

The Best Investment Money Can't Buy

What a gift to give to others!

Eric England

Introduction

As soon as you touch this book you will feel God's Love. You will want to read the whole book and you will not want to put it down. You will be blessed and will be able to bless others.

The Best Investment Money Can't Buy is a book full of messages that were written to share God's Word. These messages will speak to your heart, soul, and mind and you should share them worldwide. You will feel the power of God and you will hear him speak to you. Please tell others about this book or give it as a gift.

God speaks to us for a reason and he wants you to act on what you hear. Faith comes from hearing and hearing comes from the Word of God. This book will change your life. Don't be deceived you are in a spiritual battle every second of your life. The spiritual battle you are in every second of your life whether you like it or not is between Good and Evil. You may not even believe in God, but you are being deceived if you don't. Even evil spirits acknowledge Christ according to the Bible. Deceptions are half-truths, are you being deceived? The evil one speaks half-truths and tempts you to do what is wrong. God speaks the full truth and encourages you to do what is righteous. Satan is a liar, he wants to kill, steal, and destroy you and keep you separated from God. God cannot lie; he wants you to have eternal life with him. The evil one makes promises that he cannot keep that will lead you down the path of destruction and even death. God makes covenants that last forever that will lead you down the path of happiness and eternal life. Satan wants you to feel bad about yourself, discouraged, disappointed, and depressed. He wants you to follow him and not God. He wants you to "TRY" and find fulfillment through the flesh. Fleshly things would be sex before marriage, adultery, drugs, alcohol, pornography, lust, homosexuality, the love of money, pride, or anything that goes against God's Word and commandments. You are either righteous or you are not; this is the absolute truth. God wants you to have love, joy, peace, patience, kindness, goodness, faithfulness, gentleness, and self-control. If you are not experiencing these kinds of fruit in your life, then you better examine yourself. You are being deceived.

Get yourself a bible and read Romans 10:9-10 and do what it says, this will be the first greatest day of the rest of your life. The best way to find out the real truth is to search for it on your own. The best place to search for the truth is in the Bible. The Bible or scriptures should be used to teach, edify the saints, rebuke, correct, train in righteousness, and share the good news about God. The messages in this book use scriptures to share the truth, teach, edify the saints, rebuke, correct, train in righteousness, share the good news about God, and most importantly change your life. There is something for everyone in this book.

(Acts 20:24 New Living Translation says, "your life is worth nothing unless you use it for doing the work assigned you by the Lord Jesus–the work of telling others the Good

News about God's wonderful kindness and love").[1] For many be called, but few chosen.

I was called to write these messages and you have been called to read them and chosen to share them with others. This book will change your life, you will be blessed and be able to bless others. You did not pick this book up by chance; there was a reason why you picked it up. God wants a relationship with you, he wants to bless you and bless you abundantly so you can do the same for others. You have been called to be a servant, to serve others just like Jesus served. Please do not be deceived and act on your temptations (fleshly things) and follow Satan, your life will be miserable. You will never find total fulfillment in anything unless you have Christ in your life and do what he says to do. Having Jesus as your Lord and Savior is "The Best Investment That Money Can't Buy". Meditate on these messages and put them into action, and more importantly share them with others. God is speaking to you for a reason. God is preparing you for something that is about to happen and you can help prepare others. Stay alert, be on your toes, and do not take things for granted, God has a reason for what you hear, see, and do. He has called people to do the things you need to hear, see, and do. These people are speaking what needs to be heard, showing what needs to be seen, and doing what needs to be done. God has always used people to complete his plan and his plan will be completed. Stop being deceived. You are in a spiritual battle. This is a life or death choice. Put sin to death. You are being called; please act on this calling.

Answer the questions after each reading before going on to the next message. Watch and listen to what God reveals to you, you will be amazed how the Spirit works.

CONTENTS

We Are The Chosen "Ones"..15

Are You Ready? 17

Question Yourself To Get Out Of Spiritual And

Financial Debt..20

What Is Church And Why Do You Need The Bible?.........32

Strengthening Our Belief: Why And How?......................42

We Are In The Age Of Fulfillment...................................49

No Retirement..54

Temple Tampering 56

Revival To Salvation—Why Isn't It Happening?.............58

Nothing Means Nothing! 63

What To Do Next 67

But You Can't See God, But You Can't See Satan
Either, Or Can We See Both?.........................71

How Beautiful We Are With Our Eyes Closed.................80

Easy—Hard.......................84

Good News-Bad News.....................93

We Are Like Trees...........................100

Weather The Storm 102

Unemployed And Out Of Work 104

Pity Party........................108

The Right Person For The Job!.......................111

Get Excited About Your Calling 115

Conclusion: Honor God 119

We Are The Chosen "Ones"

We are the ones in the battle, the ones wanting to serve, the ones chosen to save the lost, the ones who love the sinner and hold fast to the Word and doctrine of God. When you are chosen, how do you feel, does it make you happy? When you are not chosen how do you feel? God has some words of wisdom for you:

- I see you...fix your eyes on what is not seen, not what you can see; the things of this world, they will lead you down the path of destruction.

- I hear you...fix your ears on what is not heard, not what you can hear; the things of this world, they will lead you down the path of destruction.

- I know you…fix your knowledge on the Mystery of God what is not known, not what you can know; the things of this world, they will lead you down the path of destruction.

We are like White Flags, i.e. the Chosen Ones-we have surrendered to God, we are pure and cleansed. Others are like Red Flags, i.e. the Lost Ones-they have not surrendered to God, they are not pure and cleansed yet! They are chosen. Who by? The Evil One! They believe the devil's half-truths and live unhappy lives, they are being deceived, but they can become White Flags by surrendering to God, by hearing the call, the call is now! Surrender to him before it is too late; you are not promised tomorrow, be one of the Chosen "Ones". God will speak the truth to you; do you see him calling, do you hear him calling, and do you know he is calling? The choice is yours.

What has God revealed to you so far? Have you chosen Him? You have been chosen, are you ready?

Are You Ready?

W hy do you need to hear the Word of God preached? The Bible says there will be a time when people will not listen to the Word of God because of their own desires. You need to be thoroughly equipped and you do this by knowing and hearing the scriptures or the Word of God. (2 Timothy 3:16-17) **16** All Scripture is given by inspiration of God, and is profitable for doctrine, for reproof, for correction, for instruction in righteousness, **17** that the man of God may be complete, thoroughly equipped for every good work. You are called and chosen to fulfill your ministry by preaching the Word of God and evangelizing to the lost.

Are you ready? You should be ready all the time! For nobody knows the time nor the hour that the Lord will come back! "You have received the Spirit from the Holy One and all of us know the Truth. The Truth is that you have been anointed by God and have an unction to function. You have an unction to function, but you need to start functioning. This function is to change the world and save the lost. You function by witnessing to the lost not inside the church, but outside the walls of the church. You need to learn how to function and to move in the anointing and power that God has given you. You need to function in the power of God. How do you function in the power of God? Learning the mystery of God, prayer, laying on of hands, fasting, pressing forth and preaching and teaching the Word of God boldly, doing things in the name of Jesus, being filled with the Holy Spirit, sharing what you own and giving witness that the Lord Jesus has risen from the dead, stretching out your hands to heal and doing miraculous signs and wonders through the name of our holy servant Jesus."[2]

God will anoint you and give you the Words to speak, just as he has given me the words to write in these messages. The church itself has many members (the body) that should be using their gifts and talents and causing the church to function as one. It is time to get ready and have the unction to function. It is time to be ready and spread the good news. Start functioning! (Luke 4:18-19) **18** "The Spirit of the LORD is upon Me, Because He has anointed Me To preach the gospel to the poor; He has sent Me to heal the broken-hearted, To proclaim liberty to the captives And recovery of sight to the blind, To set at liberty those who are oppressed; **19** To proclaim the acceptable year of the LORD."

You have been chosen, are you ready? What are you waiting for? Question yourself to get out of spiritual and financial debt?

Question Yourself To Get Out Of Spiritual And Financial Debt

Write your answers in the space provided.

Why do you come to church or why should you being going to church?

What are you expecting when you're at church?

What are you taking with you when you leave church?

Who are you listening to during the message?

When are you going to put what you hear into Action?

Where are you going to put what you hear into Action?

Do you question yourself and self-examine yourself daily to see where you are at in your walk with God?

Are you denying self and taking up your cross daily to follow Christ?

Are you properly conducting yourself in your actions and attitudes?

Has God shown you what is righteous and good?

Do you do what is right?

Do you have mercy for others?

Do you humble yourself?

Do you have unconditional love for others?

Are you continually preparing yourself?

Are you fully dedicating yourself to God?

Are you fully committed to God?

Are you calling out to God for His guidance?

Are you praying to Him on a daily basis and doing intercessory prayer for others?

Are you experiencing these kinds of fruit in your life; love, joy, peace, patience, kindness, goodness, faithfulness, gentleness, and self-control?

Do you think you are in a spiritual battle?

What do you think your life is all about?

Do you need a life changing experience?

Are you in spiritual and financial debt?

The Church, the government, the state, the world, and maybe even you are in spiritual and financial debt today. Why are we in spiritual and financial debt? The answer is simple but it is very confusing. It is simple but confusing because God's ways are not our ways!

We are living in the last days, which could be another 2,000 years or it could be in a blink of an eye. After all, how old is the Bible and how many times does it talk about the end times and Jesus coming back soon? See this is very simple but confusing, this is God's way. You must believe, love, and cast off the works of darkness because nobody knows the time nor the hour that Christ will return for his Church.

(Romans 13:8-14) **8** Owe no one anything except to love one another, for he who loves another has fulfilled the law. **9** For the commandments, "You shall not commit adultery," "You shall not murder," "You shall not steal," "You shall not bear false witness," "You shall not covet," and if there is any other commandment, are all summed up in this saying, namely, "You shall love your neighbor as yourself." **10** Love does no harm to a neighbor; therefore love is the fulfillment of the law. **11** And do this, knowing the time, that now it is high time to awake out of sleep; for now our salvation is nearer than when we first believed. **12** The night is far spent, the day is at hand. Therefore let us cast off the works of darkness, and let us put on the armor of light. **13** Let us walk properly, as in the day, not in revelry and drunkenness, not in lewdness and lust, not in strife and envy. **14** But put on the Lord Jesus Christ, and make no provision for the flesh, to fulfill its lusts.

One reason we are in spiritual and financial debt is because we are not stirred up for God. We are not obedient to God. We are not submissive to God. We do not put God first in everything we do. We do not wisely manage what God has given us. Read Matthew 25, Luke 12, I Corinthians 3, Proverbs 11, 13, and 21. We are not investing in diverse resources. God wants you to manage your resources wisely. You need spiritual wisdom because wisdom will guide you. Ask God for wisdom just like Solomon did. We are not using our gifts. It is time to stir up the gifts, stir up the Spirit, build a fire inside of you, get radical for God; this is the answer, this is the starting point.

Secondly, put your confidence in God. The more confidence in God, the more confidence you will have in yourself. It is time for redemption. See this is another simple but confusing way of God; I sin but someone else dies for me and now my sin is washed away? Redemption converts you back to God. It is time to convert back to the storehouse of God!

See, getting out of spiritual and financial debt is simple but confusing. We live in a Charge All society when we should be living in a Cash All society. A Charge All society means: buy what you want now and pay for it later or for the rest of your life; the latter for most of society. A Cash All society means you do not buy what you want unless you have the money to pay for it. NOW ISN'T THAT SIMPLE? Now charging isn't bad, as a matter of fact it is wise; once again simple but confusing. You can charge what you NEED on your credit card and invest your money for another one to two months before you have to pay the bill. Also, if you pay with a credit card you make one payment for all purchases and you can see where you have been spending your money; this is wisdom. Now it is wise if you have the money to pay off the balance and unwise if you don't. If you can't pay off the balance you will be in spiritual and financial debt and will be paying high interest payments instead of making interest. If you can't manage your credit card and pay off the balance each month when it is due you should cut up your credit card and throw it away and use the Cash All proven method. A Charge All society is man's way not God's way. Our government is a great poor example of this. If you follow the government example you definitely are going to be in spiritual and financial debt and that is the way the government wants you to be; indebted to it! After all, how many trillions of dollars is our government in debt? What about spiritual debt? The government continues to take God out of everything when God should be the center of everything! Believers better get some wisdom. The world better get some wisdom or we will all be in spiritual and financial debt.

Lastly, if you want to get out of spiritual and financial debt and be blessed abundantly, start giving. Now that is simple but confusing. Get out of spiritual and financial debt by giving? (II Corinthians 9:6-15) **6** But this I say: He who sows sparingly will also reap sparingly, and he who sows bountifully will also reap bountifully. **7** So let each one give as he purposes in his heart, not grudgingly or of necessity; for God loves a cheerful giver. **8** And God is able to make all grace abound toward you, that you, always having all sufficiency in all things, may have an abundance for every good work. **9** As it is written: He has dispersed abroad, He has given to the poor; His righteousness endures forever." **10** Now may He who supplies seed to the sower, and bread for food, supply and multiply the seed you have sown and increase the fruits of your righteousness, **11** while you are enriched in everything for all liberality, which causes thanksgiving through us to God. **12** For the administration of this service not only supplies the needs of the saints, but also is abounding through many thanksgivings to God, **13** while, through the proof of this ministry, they glorify God for the obedience of your confession to the gospel of Christ, and for your liberal sharing with them and all men, **14** and by their prayer for you, who long for you because of the exceeding grace of God in you. **15** Thanks be to God for His indescribable gift! (Proverbs 3:9-10) **9** Honor the LORD with your possessions, And with the first fruits of all your increase; **10** So your barns will be filled with plenty, And your vats will overflow with new wine.

The Bible is full of scriptures telling us the importance of giving. Giving comes from the heart and gives a great picture about your character and how much you love God and others. God really does not need you to give Him anything because He already owns it all, but wants you to give your first fruits of what He has allowed you to have so He can bless you abundantly. His storehouse makes Fort Knox look like a pebble in the sand, a needle in a haystack, His bank is everywhere, an unending money tree. So if you want more give more. Jesus gave everything so what do you think you should give?

It is time for the Church to get out of spiritual and financial debt! It is time to: stir up your gifts, get radical for God, put your confidence in God, give to God first, and ask God for wisdom to lead and guide you. Give and get out of spiritual and financial debt, simple but confusing or is it?

You have been chosen, are you ready? What are you waiting for? Question yourself and get out of spiritual and financial debt? What is church and why do you need the bible?

What Is Church And
Why Do You Need The Bible?

Church is not a building or a group of people gathering in a building. To some Church is a certain denomination, a place to go on Sunday and Wednesday, and a place to hear people preach. The fact of the matter is that none of these are the Church. The word church came from the Greek word Ekklesia. Ekklesia or Ecclesia means an assembly, to be called out, or the called out ones. Believers who have been called out of the world by God and follow Jesus Christ are the Church.

The Church is made up of a body of believers that are given gifts, to serve and meet the needs of others. The Church that includes you if you are a believer must do the will of

God, before you can do anything on your own. The Church must be the ambassador proclaiming and professing His will through Prayer, through the Word, and through the Spirit. When all parts of the body proclaim and profess His will through Prayer, through the Word, and through the Spirit the Church functions as one. The Church must function as one to edify and meet the needs of others; this is Church.

Where two or more are gathered together in His name and agree on His Word then God has to answer the prayers. The word "if" is a big word in the Bible. If you are in the Will of God everything He promises in the Word will happen. How do you get in the Will of God? Knowing the Word, the Word is the Will of God. If you pray the Will of God, he must answer. The prayer must be in complete agreement with the Will for the Power to be released. You must know the Word to know the Will of God. Nothing will happen unless it goes through the Church and the Church is God the Father, God the Son, and God the Holy Spirit equals the Trinity.

Christ or Jesus did nothing, but what God told Him to do. You must go through Christ to get to God. He is your intercessor. Mary can not intercede for you, Buddha can not intercede for you, Muhammad can not intercede for you, and Ouija Boards can not intercede for you; only Jesus can.

The Word of God has been made known through Scripture and specifically through Jesus Christ. Jesus described the importance of the Scriptures in Matthew 4:4 when he said, "Man shall not live by bread alone, but by every word that proceeds from the mouth of God". Jesus also emphasized the importance of searching the Scriptures steadfastly. John 5:39 says, You search the Scriptures for in them you think you have eternal life; and these are they which testify of Me. The Scriptures give you all the answers to all questions.

The Bible explains exactly what God expects from His church. He has explained everything that he wants done through and by the Church and what He wants accomplished throughout the world.

The church is responsible for accomplishing this world-wide mission. This world-wide mission that God wants accomplished through His Church is spreading the mystery of Christ. The way the church learns how to spread the mystery of Christ is by reading, following, and teaching the Bible.

The Bible is one way God speaks to you. As you pray and read the Bible, God reveals himself to you, he shows you what His expectations are, he is expecting a love relationship with you, he is calling you to action, and he is revealing the changes you need to make in your life.

You can have a relationship with God by reading the Bible, listening to Him, and obeying what He says. God has called you to be with Him because he loves you and he is a jealous God. God wants you to do what he has called you to do. He speaks to you individually and to His Church through the Bible, through worship, through prayer, through circumstances, through the Holy Spirit, and through Bible studies.[3]

The Bible teaches the Church what God's commandments are, what His expectations are, and what the Church should be doing so it does not depart from Him. His Word explains and gives examples how He disciplines His Church when it departs from his commands, His expectations, and for not doing what He has called the Church to do. The

Church should be crying out to Him for help and guidance in all situations. His Church should be crying out to Him on a daily basis for help and direction! You should be crying out to Him on a daily basis for help and direction.

Each part of the body is responsible for this relationship and mission with God. The body should be in a love relationship with God. The Bible provides exact choices and/or consequences in this love relationship. These exact choices and/or consequences are in God's Word for you and the Church: God's way or judgment, repent or perish. When the Church follows the Bible's teaching on repentance, there is a revival, a spiritual awakening. God revives and awakens us so He can accomplish His plan and redeem the lost outside the Church.[4] What is the Bible for? Knowing and Doing the Will of God!

The Church is the body of people God has chosen to do this. He desires to have a love relationship with His Church body. This relationship happens and can only happen through Jesus Christ. You must have faith in Jesus Christ as your

Lord and Savior, committing your life to Him, obeying Him, and doing what He has called you to do.[5]

God's chosen people, Israel, were the forerunners of the Church.[6] The Israelites are a great example for us. They were chosen to be the church model for us. How did they do? So what is Church? The Church is Jesus Christ as the Head or Chief Cornerstone who builds it (Matt 16:18) and equips and arranges it according to His will (I Cor 12:18). The Church is the living body of Jesus Christ with many uniquely equipped members (Ephesians 4:11-16) **11** And He Himself gave some to be apostles, some prophets, some evangelists, and some pastors and teachers, **12** for the equipping of the saints for the work of ministry, for the edifying of the body of Christ, **13** till we all come to the unity of the faith and of the knowledge of the Son of God, to a perfect man, to the measure of the stature of the fullness of Christ; **14** that we should no longer be children, tossed to and fro and carried about with every wind of doctrine, by the trickery of men, in the cunning craftiness of deceitful plotting, **15** but, speaking the truth in love, may grow up in all things into Him who is the head—Christ— **16** from whom the whole body, joined and knit together by what every joint supplies, according to the effective working by which every part does its share, causes growth of the body for the edifying of itself in love. The Church desires a love relationship with Jesus Christ, who is Head of the body with all things under His feet and he is Head over all things. He is Head of the Church, which is His body. Every part of the body is important. Each part of the body must do its share. When each part of the body does its share the body will grow and edify the other parts of the body.

The Church is a body of believers with many uniquely equipped members that should be in total unity. The uniqueness of believers is that they should be in an interdependent relationship with each other. God has designed this unique interdependent relationship for the equipping of the saints so they can minister to and edify the body of Christ until the body becomes one in faith and one in unity. The body has to be knowledgeable about the Son of God. Once the body becomes one in faith, one in unity, and knowledgeable about

God it can experience the fullness of Christ. God is always working and he gives the Church the gifts needed to do the work. The Church is a people always working with Christ. This work is to share the mystery of God, the mystery of the gospel.

You are reconcilers and are called to make disciples of all the nations, baptizing them in the name of the Father and of the Son and of the Holy Spirit, teaching them to observe all things that I have commanded you; and lo, I am with you always, even to the end of the age, says the Lord. (Matthew 28:19-20). The harvest is plentiful, but the workers are few.

In conclusion, what is Church and why do you need the Bible? The Church is a body of committed believers who allow God's spirit to lead and guide them so they can go throughout the world and save the lost. The Church is a servant of Christ and allows the Holy Spirit to lead it and guide it. The power comes from the Holy Spirit. The Church body should be setting the example through worship and servant-hood to edify and meet the needs of other believers and ministering to the lost. The purpose of the Church is to glorify God in everything it says and does. The body must have all the God given members to be complete. The Church is made in God's image to be holy, pure and righteous and to do what he has called the Church to do so he alone gets the glory. The body must demonstrate God's love throughout the world and to the lost. Church is Christ as the Head of the Church the Chief Cornerstone to lead and guide it and He should be Head of your life also. The Church must do the will of God "if" it wants to become one flesh with Christ and be His royal priesthood. The Church is God, Jesus, and the Holy Spirit known as the Trinity and the body should only be doing what God says to do, just as Christ only did what God told Him to do. The Church must obey and be fully committed to Him and do what he has called it to do. The body must be holy, pure, be in complete unity, and love everyone unconditionally.

The Bible tells you that you are a sinner, to repent, and confess Jesus as your Lord and Savior so that you can have eternal life with Him "if" you do what God tells you to do. The Bible offers forgiveness and you need forgiveness. The

Bible gives you a step-by-step and point-by-point analysis about yourself; who you are, what you need, and tells you the way to find fulfillment of your needs and desires. The Bible helps you bare your trials, gives you the power to resist temptation (deception), it promises you eternal life, it teaches love, it tells you that you are a friend of God, and it is the truth that will set you free. You learn these things by reading the Bible, doing bible studies, prayer, fasting, praise and worship, through your circumstances, and having fellowship with other believers. This is church and this is why you need the Bible.

You have been chosen, are you ready? What are you waiting for? Question yourself and get out of spiritual and financial debt? What is church and why do you need the bible? How and why do you strengthen your belief?

Strengthening Our Belief: Why And How?

We strengthen our belief by getting in tune with God, putting God first in everything we do. We must die to and forget self, yield the soul to Him completely. When we die to and forget self and yield the soul to Him completely, our soul finds and touches Christ. Belief is to have faith and faith is the substance of things hoped for and the evidence of things not seen (Hebrews 11:1). Faith requires constant attention and work. Where does faith come from? (Romans 10:17) So then faith comes by hearing and hearing from the Word of God.

Scripture is called The Word of God, Oracles of God, Sword of the Spirit, and we know it as the Bible. The

Scriptures are given by the inspiration of God and the Holy Spirit or Holy Ghost (II Timothy 3:16, Acts 1:16, Hebrews 3:7, and II Peter 1:21). While Christ was on earth he taught the Scriptures and used them against His spiritual enemies (Matthew 4:4, Mark 12:10, John 7:42, and Luke 24:27).[7]

The Scriptures contain the promises of God, the laws of God, the commandments and judgments of God, the prophecies of God and most importantly explains who Christ is (Romans 1:2, Deuteronomy 4:5 & 14, II Peter 1:19-21, John 5:39, Acts 10:43, Acts 18:28, and I Corinthians 15:3). The Scriptures are everything we need, completely true and without error. The Scriptures lead us to Christ so we can receive our salvation and we do this through faith and confession that Jesus Christ died and rose again and is now Lord of our life (Romans 10:9-10, Luke 16:29-31, Proverbs 6:23, and II Timothy 3:10-15).[8]

We need Scriptures because they are truth and the truth will set you free, they cut like a two-edge sword, they are pure as gold and teach us to be pure, they are precious like silver and we are precious in the eyes of God, they are perfect and we are to be perfected through them, and they are powerful beyond belief and we receive our power through them. Scriptures are quick like lightening, illuminating like the moon, are for converting the soul, sanctifying your life, and reconciling you to Him (John 6:63, John 17:17, John 20:31, Romans 15:4, I Peter 1:23, James 1:16-18, Psalm 19:7, Psalm 19:10, Psalm 119, Ephesians 5:26, and Hebrews 4:12). The Scriptures produce faith, hope, and love. Scripture teaches us to be obedient, scripture will cleanse the heart, scripture is for converting the soul, and scripture teaches us to be wise (John 15:3, John 20:31, Romans 15:4, I Corinthians 13:13, Deuteronomy 17:19-20). The Scriptures should be the blue print of your life. Believe what they say, yearn for them, read them daily, know and do what the Scriptures say. Most importantly read them and teach them publicly to all. Put the Word into your heart, soul, and mind and obey it. Although you should yearn and desire to hear the Word of God, you should not only hear it, but do what it says (I Peter 4:11, John 2:22, I Corinthians 1:31, II Timothy 3:15, I Thessalonians 2:13, James 1:21, and Deuteronomy 6:6).[9]

You learn and know the Word of God so you can use it against your spiritual enemies. The Word should be the most important thing in your life, your passion, your sword, your bread, and your guide. You should yearn and desire to read the Word, to mediate on the Word daily, gain wisdom and understanding from the Word, and receive the fruits from the Word (Matthew 4:4-7, Matthew 7:24, Deuteronomy 17:19, Nehemiah 8:1, Job 23:12, and Psalm 119).[10]

Therefore, put the Word in your heart, put your hope in the Word, meditate on the Word daily, definitely put all your trust in the Word, and most importantly always obey what the Word says.[11] Tell about the Word whenever you can. Pray and be conformed by the Word. Confess the Word's promises when you pray, when you fast, when healing people, and edify others. Use the Word or Scriptures for everything (Psalm 119).

Trust and obedience are major factors in strengthening our belief or faith. The Word tells us to trust and obey because there isn't any other way. The type of trust and obedience I am talking about is committing your whole soul, mind, and body to Christ. The best way to completely understand what I am talking about is to read Hebrews 11. This will give you a total understanding of trust, obedience, and belief or faith. When you trust Christ he will forgive and cleanse you, he will become your friend.

Here are some keys to strengthening your faith: listen to the Word of God every chance you get. What goes into you is what programs you and what you read or listen to affects what you believe. Realize that God has given every believer a measure of faith. You must continue to put your faith into action. Prayer is very important in strengthening your faith, Jesus prayed whenever he could. Obeying God and doing what he says to do will strengthen your faith. Facing trials and tribulations will really strengthen your faith. He convicts you when you are not obeying him to help strengthen your faith. He does miracles to strengthen your faith. Trusting God completely in any and all situations will strengthen your faith.

You are tested all the time and may not even realize it; your life is a test. God wants you to grow, but he will not allow more than you can handle. If you are faithful in little things then and only then can you be faithful in big things. Believe things before they happen and do not doubt, the Word says give thanks always and in all situations.

Praise and worship is an act of faith and expresses our love to God. Fellowship and surround yourself with the most spiritual people you know; church is a great place to go to do this. If you are not or will not go to church here on earth, what do you think you are going to do in Heaven? Heaven is church all the time! Your excuses for not participating on earth will not suffice in Heaven. Matter of fact, your excuses here on earth will not get you to Heaven. God's Word says that he will be sending Jesus Christ back for His Church and you better be part of it now if you want to be part of it later. You say you don't need Church? The answer to that statement is you don't need to go to Heaven!

Strengthening your belief starts by obeying God and His Word. This shows that you truly love God and trust Him. Faith pleases God and one day He will say "well done good and faithful servant". Read the Word, pray, be thankful for trials and tribulations, praise and worship Him, and fellowship with other believers. These things will completely strengthen you and you will find peace, joy, and love that you have never encountered before. When the time comes, you will be able to say, "It is finished" and I ran a good race.

You have been chosen, are you ready? What are you waiting for? Question yourself and get out of spiritual and financial debt? What is church and why do you need the bible? How and why do you strengthen your belief? Are you in the age of fulfillment?

We Are In The Age Of Fulfillment

W e must escape the corruption of the world, lustful worldly corruption. We should be sharing a new divine life. This new divine life is Salvation. How do we do this? We do this by Faith. Faith needs constant attention and work. II Peter 1:6-10 says, and I am paraphrasing: add to faith Virtue and to virtue Knowledge, and to knowledge Temperance, and to temperance Patience, and to patience Godliness, and to godliness Brotherly Kindness and brotherly kindness Charity. Without these seven things we are shortsighted, even unto blindness, we have forgotten that we were cleansed from our old sins. If we do these seven things we will never stumble. God is expecting us to develop good fruit and share our fruits with others.

Everyone produces a life of works. These works are either good or they are bad, Godly or Worldly. Some will say Lord, Lord, but Jesus will say he never knew them. Why, because they have not done the Will of the Father who is in heaven. A person can prophesy, cast out demons, and do many miraculous things in the Lords name and still not make it to heaven. Why? They practice lawlessness or sin. How do we keep this from happening to us? We must hear the Word of God and more importantly we must do what it says. We must be Doers of the Word. Read the book of James.

Our foundation is like the foundation of a house, it is the most important part of the building; our foundation must be built on God's Word and we must always do what the Word tells us to do. If we hear and do not do what his Word says, we will fall and it will be a great fall. Read Matthew 7:21-27. The Word is very clear about this in Mark 4:3-20. When Jesus spoke a parable: Verse 15 basically says that we hear the Word, but we are taken away by Satan. Verse 16-17 basically says we hear the Word, receive it, but we do not have any root and it only lasts for a short time. Verse 18-19 says that we hear the Word, but it is choked out and we are unfruitful. Verse 20 says that we hear the Word, accept it, and we produce a crop. We can all get to verse twenty it is your choice!

How do we demonstrate true Faith? We demonstrate true Faith through obedience to God's revealed Will. Genuine Faith always seeks the opportunity of doing what is good and righteous. Faith proves itself in works. The opposite of doing good and being righteous can happen if we are tempted and act on the temptation. What is temptation? Temptation is when something captures our attention and induces us to do evil. We then choose to act on the temptation or not to act on the temptation. If we choose to act on the temptation we sin. We sin when we put "self" first before Christ and forget our Christian teachings and ethics.

Can you resist temptation? James 1:12 – Blessed is the man who endures temptation; for when he has been approved, he will receive the crown of life which the Lord has promised to those who love Him. Can you endure the trials? What trials will you face? Trials on how you put Faith into action, trials on whether your daily conversations witness to God, trials on how you relate to people that you have been taught to hate, trials to give up your pride; how much pride will you sacrifice to Him? Other trials you may face are trials to test your desire for and use of material possessions.

Do you have a correct attitude toward the Word of God? Do you listen to God speak and do what he says? Is God at work in your life right now, what is He calling you to do? Are you doing what He has called you to do? Will you let your prayer life be the road map of everything you do? What is your foundation made up of? Is it a strong foundation?

We are in the age of fulfillment, how can you produce Spiritual Fruit? You can produce Spiritual Fruit by controlling your tongue, choosing between wealth and God, not being prejudice, deepening your faith through and by God, being a doer of the Word, and being obedient.

You should always be in the presence of God and be sensitive to His leading when you read Scriptures, pray, or praise and worship Him. What have you seen, heard, and learned from him so far? Can you sense His presence? Has he spoken to you? Has he called you? Can you see where he is working in your life as you read these messages? Where is God working in your life today, are you there with Him? Is God testing or disciplining you, do you know? How are you going to respond to Him? Are you expecting God to act when you are praying, does this book and what you do on a daily basis lead you to action for God? Are your words edifying and blessing other people? Are you chasing worldly and materialistic things and allowing yourself to be separated from God? Are you letting these things separate you from God? Are you in faith paralysis? We should be spreading the Word and we should be yielding completely to God. Let's share the divine life and be fulfilled in Christ and Christ alone. He wants you to join Him. We are in the age of fulfillment. Amen.

You have been chosen, are you ready? What are you waiting for? Question yourself and get out of spiritual and financial debt? What is church and why do you need the bible? How and why do you strengthen your belief? Are you in the age of fulfillment, what are you filling yourself up with? Is there retirement with God?

No Retirement

God is not finished with you yet. Oh, you may think he is. You may think you've peaked. You may think he has someone else to do the job. If so, think again. God began doing a good work in you, and I am sure he will continue that work in you until it is finished. It will be finished when Jesus Christ comes again (Philippians 1:6). Do you see what God is doing? God is doing a good work in you. Do you know when he will be finished? He will be finished when Jesus comes again. May I spell out the message? God isn't finished with you yet! Pay attention to what is happening each day, God is doing something somewhere, do not take it for granted, there is a reason. Your eyes are open, but you are not watching and some of you are not praying.

Our work for the Lord is not done until Jesus comes back. We are never in retirement when it comes to the Lord. And what does he promise to us if we continue to be faithful and do his work? He promises a long life called eternity. You should be watching and praying; remember you are never in retirement when it comes to the Lord!

You have been chosen, are you ready? What are you waiting for? Question yourself and get out of spiritual and financial debt? What is church and why do you need the bible? How and why do you strengthen your belief? Are you in the age of fulfillment, what are you filling yourself up with? Is there retirement with God? What is your temple?

Temple Tampering

Did you know that you are God's temple and that God's Spirit lives in you? If anyone destroys God's temple, God will destroy that person, because God's temple is holy and you are that temple (I Cor 3:16), be careful how you feed it, use it, and maintain it. You would not want someone trashing or misusing your home; God does not want anyone trashing or misusing His. After all, it is His, isn't it? As for me and my house, we will serve the Lord (Joshua 24:15).

You are violating the temple of God and violating your sister or brother when you have sex with them outside of marriage, or do drugs with them, or get drunk with them. You are to be protecting and not violating the temple. You need to be protecting God's children and temple, not violating them. You are violating the temple and a child of God when you get them to lie, steal, cheat, talk filthy, and act worldly. You need to STOP violating and start protecting. Do what is right and not what is wrong. God knows what you are doing and he wants you to STOP, REPENT and be CLEANSED. Wake up Oh sinner and hear my voice and know that I am God. You need to stop, stop now, you vipers. It is time to act like the children of God, hear what I am saying and repent, be cleansed in Jesus name! Read about John the Baptist in Matthew chapter three.

You have been chosen, are you ready? What are you waiting for? Question yourself and get out of spiritual and financial debt? What is church and why do you need the bible? How and why do you strengthen your belief? Are you in the age of fulfillment, what are you filling yourself up with? Is there retirement with God? What is your temple? Are revivals causing salvations today?

REVIVAL TO SALVATION — WHY ISN'T IT HAPPENING?

Salvation is not just a narrow escape from hell. What was shed on us abundantly was that we should be made heirs, heirs of God and joint heirs with Christ (Romans 8:16-17). What a "great salvation". Do not neglect salvation. (Hebrews 2:1-4) **1** Therefore we must give the more earnest heed to the things we have heard, lest we drift away. **2** For if the word spoken through angels proved steadfast, and every transgression and disobedience received a just reward, **3** how shall we escape if we neglect so great a salvation, which at the first began to be spoken by the Lord, and was confirmed to us by those who heard Him, **4** God also bearing witness both with signs and wonders, with various miracles, and gifts of the Holy Spirit, according to His own will?

God is waiting for the Church to become "One" unified all together without division, denomination, deception, death, and divorce. God puts the gifts in the Church so that they might prepare God's people to serve. If it is done God's way, the body of Christ will be built up. The body will continue to grow until we all become one in the faith and in the knowledge of God's Son. Then and only then will we be grown up in the faith and be able to receive everything that Christ has for us.

Division, denomination, deception, death, and divorce start with D; so does Devil. When we are not "One" we are separated from Christ, this means we are divided into parts, kept apart, put in different categories, and going different ways.[12] Satan wants division in the church and church family. Man chooses a way to be identified and have different ideas meaning a denomination which can lead to separation from the universal church that Jesus will be coming back for. Deception is a major tool used to keep us apart so we do not function as "One", we are mislead just like Adam and Eve. Sin causes us to be dead and separated from Christ and could be causing others to be dead also. Satan especially likes us to be divorced from each other, the Church, our family, and our spouse. Divorce means the complete separation of things.[13] It is time for the church to get rid of the "D's" and concentrate on the "U's"; the unified, universal, and unveiled Church of Christ (Us). Ephesians 4 explains this very clearly: I, therefore, the prisoner of the Lord, beseech you to walk worthy of the calling with which you were called, with all lowliness and gentleness, with longsuffering, bearing with one another in love, endeavoring to keep the unity of the Spirit in the bond of peace. There is one body and one Spirit, just as you were called in one hope of your calling; one Lord, one faith, one baptism; one God and Father of all, who is above all, and through all, and in you all. But to each one of us grace was given according to the measure of Christ's gift. And He Himself gave some to be apostles, some prophets, some evangelists, and some pastors and teachers, for the equipping of the saints for the work of ministry, for the edifying of the body of Christ, till we all come to the unity of the faith and of the knowledge of the Son of God, to a perfect man, to the measure of the stature of the fullness of Christ; that we should no longer be children, tossed to and fro and carried about with every wind of doctrine, by the trickery of men, in the cunning craftiness of deceitful plotting, but, speaking the truth in love, may grow up in all things into Him who is the head—Christ—from whom the whole body, joined and knit together by what every joint supplies, according to the effective working by which every part does its share, causes growth of the body for the edifying of itself in love.

Acts 2:46 says, they continued daily with one accord in the temple, and breaking bread from house to house, did eat their meat with gladness and singleness of heart, praising God, and having favor with all the people. And the Lord added to the Church daily such as should be saved. Does the Church want true revival? Act 2:1-47 gives us the simple answer.

We should be living in the light explained by Ephesians 5. We must do the will of God from the heart and put on the full armor of God explained in Ephesians 6. True revival will lead to salvations when we start doing what Acts 5:42 tells us to do; daily in the temple, and in every house, we should not cease to teach and preach Jesus Christ. Amen-So Be It!

You have been chosen, are you ready? What are you waiting for? Question yourself and get out of spiritual and financial debt? What is church and why do you need the bible? How and why do you strengthen your belief? Are you in the age of fulfillment, what are you filling yourself up with? Is there retirement with God? What is your temple? Are revivals causing salvations today? What is important to you?

Nothing Means Nothing!

Today, there are many things out on the Internet and emails that say, "If you send this to a certain amount of people in a certain amount of time you will receive something and if you do not something could happen to you?" You need to be careful of these emails; our only hope is in Christ and in Christ alone. One thing for sure you can count on is being obedient to Christ and sharing the gospel and/or testimonies with others and being a blessing to others and being blessed yourself. This only happens through Christ also. Christ must be the center of everything we do and then you will be blessed.

I would like to share a life changing experience with you and hopefully it will bless you and you will want to bless others with your testimony or you may send mine to others you know, especially family members who are not saved or are not following Christ. I would like to share my experience from my mission trip that was life changing and eye opening with you and others. The ultimate thing I learned from the mission trip was that the only and real importance in life is "Christ in ours". We would really like to see all our family members following and obeying Christ. One day soon God will ask everyone one simple question, what have you done in my name? That is why it is so important to have a daily examination of ones self and to be following the Word of God completely.

One of the most important parts of following His Word is to obey His commands. The other is to be part of the body to fellowship, edify, and lift each other up; this is called Church. When one part of the body is missing the body does not work to its fullest potential. We are called to worship God and share the gospel with others; these are the two main and most important goals we should have in our lives. God is waiting for His church to become unified and become as one; this is starting to happen all over the world. We saw evidence of this in Africa.

Each day is a new day and we have a choice to do many things that God desires and commands from us: (1) Love God with all your heart, soul and mind through praise and worship. (2) Love your neighbor as you love yourself with unconditional love. (3) Be righteous or in the right standing with God meaning to be Christ like in everything you say and do. (4) Trust and obey the Word of God, be a doer of the Word. (5) Be a servant and use your gifts that God has given you to help meet the needs of others. (6) Follow all the commandments in His Word. (7) Pray every chance you get. (8) Daily tell the world about the mystery of Christ. Nothing else has any importance in life and we can do absolutely nothing in our own strength; God enables us to do what we do and everything comes from God. We came into this world with nothing and we will definitely leave this world with nothing.

My new slogan from my experience in Africa is: Nothing means Nothing and Nothing is Important; We Can Be Joyful with Nothing if WE HAVE CHRIST who is EVERYTHING. That is my goal for my family and every person on earth "that they know and follow Christ". If this would happen, life on this earth would be a great place to be for a short time and Heaven will be even greater for eternity.

Until that glorious moment comes, God expects us to be Praying, Fasting, Worshipping Him, Learning His Word, and Telling Others the Mystery and Good News of Christ. We hope you will continue to do this with these messages or your own testimony. You will bless others and you will be blessed. Hopefully this will change your life as it has mine.

You have been chosen, are you ready? What are you waiting for? Question yourself and get out of spiritual and financial debt? What is church and why do you need the bible? How and why do you strengthen your belief? Are you in the age of fulfillment, what are you filling yourself up with? Is there retirement with God? What is your temple? Are revivals causing salvations today? What is important to you? What should you do after receiving salvation?

What To Do Next

When a person finally receives salvation as we hope you have by now, everyone is very happy and joyful at that moment and maybe even for a few weeks or months afterwards, but what happens next?

This time of a person's life is very important and vulnerable. We lead people to Christ and they receive Him and then everyone goes their separate direction. Direction is exactly what should be happening next. We should be directing the new Christian into the fullness of God.

The first step is teaching the new convert about baptism and getting them baptized. This teaching should be from the Bible and baptism should be done when the new convert fully understands why they are being baptized.

New Christians need a support system because they are vulnerable to Satan even more than they were before they were saved. Satan now has a legitimate reason to kill, steal, and destroy one of God's creations and a new creature "You". He will do anything he can to take you away from God. That is why it is very important to have a support system for new converts. The support system should consist of: The Word or Bible, discipleship, an elder and someone you can be accountable to and confide in, a study group, a prayer group, the church, and fellow Christians to hang out with.

Your walk with Christ should be a daily and moment-by-moment relationship. The key to this relationship is to get in tune with God as much as you can. You get in tune with God by reading the Word, praying, fasting, cleansing the heart daily, and putting Christ first in everything you do. This is called being on fire for God; to hunger and thirst for His righteousness. He will fill your hunger and your thirst; he is the bread, the water, and the life.

The Word is very clear that our faith needs constant attention and work. You should be maturing each and every day, growing daily in the things of God. Your body is now the temple of God and you should be using it to edify and bring others to Christ.

Each person has a calling on their life. You should be asking God to reveal your calling to you. **You are now very unique and different from the rest of the world and you need to understand this and be prepared that things will now be different**. Your family and maybe even your best friends will not understand this change in you and will try and drag you down, but you have to stand firm and be **Bold** for the Lord. You must now rely on the Lord and not your own understanding. Always put the Lord first in everything you do. Remember that your Christian walk will not be easy and that is why it is very important to surround yourself with a support system mentioned above. You must be sensitive to God's leading and listen to His voice. These are some very important things you should be doing each and every day, what should you do next?

You have been chosen, are you ready? What are you waiting for? Question yourself and get out of spiritual and financial debt? What is church and why do you need the bible? How and why do you strengthen your belief? Are you in the age of fulfillment, what are you filling yourself up with? Is there retirement with God? What is your temple? Are revivals causing salvations today? What is important to you? What should you do after receiving salvation? Can you see good and evil?

But You Can't See God, But You Can't See Satan Either, Or Can We See Both?

O ne day I was telling a young man about God, yes he was a lost and dying soul. He was listening to what I had to say and responded a short time into the conversation, "but you can't see God". I have experienced this response before when ministering, especially when ministering to our youth.

My response to that statement was I see God every-where: the trees, the clouds, the planets, the oceans, and every person, even you. God created everything and God is everywhere. The young man that I was ministering to had to leave and after he left God gave me this message. Yes, you can't visibly see God, but you can't visibly see Satan either, or can we see both?

God's Word says that we are made in His image, so if we are made in His image technically we can see God. God is Spirit and His Spirit is everywhere. The Spirit of God is wholly righteous and good. This kind of Spirit produces righteous fruit. Angels are a product of the good Spirit to help us and protect us. Satan was created by God, but tried to put himself above God and was kicked out of heaven. He was a fallen angel and his name is Lucifer. Lucifer or an evil spirit roams around the earth trying to kill, steal, and destroy. Demons are a product of the evil spirit to lead you down the path of destruction. How do we know Satan exist? Read Genesis 3:1-15.

Can you see good in this world? Can you see evil in this world? Yes, we can see both good and evil. (2 Corinthians 4:4) The devil who rules this world has blinded the minds of those who do not believe. They cannot see the light of the Good News-the Good News about the glory of Christ, who is exactly like God. The bottom line is you have to believe in one or the other and the one you believe in is the one you will serve. If it is not of God it is sin. Sin separates you from God and you do evil and wicked things. Genesis 6:11 says, people on earth did what God said was evil, and violence was everywhere. Can you see any violence in the world today?

You are either led by the flesh or led by the Spirit. Your flesh is contrary to your spirit and you are in a constant fight to control your evil desires because the flesh wars against the spirit. If you are led by the flesh the works are very evident according to Galatians 5:19-21. The works of the flesh are: adultery, fornication, uncleanness, lewdness, idolatry, sorcery, hatred, contentions, jealousies, outbursts of wrath, selfish ambitions, dissensions, heresies, envy, murders, drunkenness, revelries, and the like. Mark 7:21-23 says, all these things begin inside people, in the mind: evil thoughts, sexual sins, stealing, murder, adultery, greed, evil actions, lying, doing sinful things, jealousy, speaking evil of others, pride, and foolish living. All these evil things come from inside and make people unclean. Have you seen any of these? Better yet have you done any of these works of the flesh? The evil one is trying to pull you his way because he is very proud and pride will lead you down the road of destruction! Have you ever seen this happen?

The good news is God is calling you right now and he is speaking to you. Can you see Him or hear Him? Not visibly or audibly, but He is there. John 14:15-17 says. If you love me, keep my commandments. And I will pray the Father, and He will give you another Helper, that He may abide with you forever—the Spirit of truth, whom the world cannot receive, because it neither sees Him nor knows Him; but you know Him, for He dwells with you and will be in you.

If God doesn't exist why have there been so many people throughout history that believe there is a God? God created everything and everything he has created is perfect. Let's look at the earth, it is the only planet that is able to sustain life; perfect make-up of gases, perfect distance from the sun so we don't freeze or burn up. What about the moon? It is also the perfect size and located perfectly for our gravitational pull. The moon keeps our oceans in check so they don't cover all the land. It also creates tides so the oceans do not get stagnate.[14] Water the main sustainer of life, where does it come from? The wind, where does it come from? If you will research these two awesome things that God has designed you will be simply amazed what they do and how they do it.

The human body is incredibly designed and made. Think about how a human body develops. First you have to have a male and a female to be able to reproduce. Where did males and females come from? God made Adam and then God made Eve from one of Adams ribs and Adam called her woman because she was from man. The male has to have intercourse with the female to leave sperm that swims to find the one and only one female egg in the fallopian tube. This process has to be at a specific time in order for fertilization to take place. Women only have a specific number of eggs from birth and that is incredible if you really think about it! Once fertilization takes place the fetus then develops body parts, how does this Happen? The body parts are very unique and sophisticated, where did they come from? There are a thousand questions we can ask about the human body, but the only answer that can explain this complex, unique, and sophisticated make-up of a human being is God created it.

God has revealed himself through the earth, the planets, animals, the oceans, nature in general, and especially in human life. The main place that God has revealed himself is in the Bible.[15] The Bible explains everything and we can prove it is true through prophecy. The prophecy in the Bible has never been wrong; if it is wrong just one time then you could have an argument that there isn't a God. Read Psalms 22:12-18 this tells about the crucifixion a thousand years before Jesus was born and in fact crucifixion had not ever been done when that was prophesized. They did not even know what crucifixion was![16] There are many prophecies that have been fulfilled and there are some that are going to be fulfilled in the future. The way you find out is to get into the Word and listen to what God tells you. Hopefully your eyes have been opened now and you can clearly see that there is a God and unfortunately there is evil. You have daily choices to make and here are some of them that I call God versus Satan:

God vs. Satan

God wants you to read the Bible versus Satan doesn't want you to read the bible

God wants you to pray versus Satan doesn't want you to pray

God wants you to fast versus Satan doesn't want you to fast

God wants you to write what you learn versus Satan doesn't want you to write what you learn

God wants you to be obedient versus Satan wants you to be disobedient

God wants you to lift each other up versus Satan wants you to put each other down

God wants you to be accountable to each other versus Satan wants you to do your own thing

God wants you to be a servant versus Satan wants you to be selfish

God wants you to have fruits of the Spirit versus Satan wants you to have fruits of the flesh

God wants you to be righteous versus Satan wants you to be unrighteous

God wants you to worship Him versus Satan wants you to worship him

The reality of this message is that good always overcomes evil and you have to decide what path you are going to choose, (Good = God) or (Evil = Satan). Understand that the end result whether you can see either God or Satan is (Eternal Life = Heaven) or (Eternal Death = Hell) hopefully you can see that. It is not about seeing, but about believing. Believe one thing, if you do not believe in God you are playing Russian roulette with your life. One day soon you will definitely see and be one place or the other. Open your eyes and see the light. Open your ears and hear the Word. God has some words of wisdom for you:

- I see you...fix your eyes on what is not seen, not what you can see; the things of this World, they will lead you down the path of destruction.

- I hear you...fix your ears on what is not heard, not what you can hear; the things of this World, they will lead you down the path of destruction.
- I know you...fix your knowledge on the Mystery of God what is not known, not what you can know; the things of this World, they will lead you down the path of destruction.

What do you see, hear, and know now? What are you going to do about it? Truth or Consequences?

You have been chosen, are you ready? What are you waiting for? Question yourself and get out of spiritual and financial debt? What is church and why do you need the bible? How and why do you strengthen your belief? Are you in the age of fulfillment, what are you filling yourself up with? Is there retirement with God? What is your temple? Are revivals causing salvations today? What is important to you? What should you do after receiving salvation? Can you see good and evil? What do you see with your eyes closed and what do you hear with your eyes closed?

How Beautiful We Are With Our Eyes Closed

Would we look at things the same way with our eyes closed? What we see might be totally 1,000 percent different. Our perception is skewed when our eyes are open, but unbelievably not skewed when our eyes are closed. Why can't we look at things the same way with our eyes open? Maybe it is because things are not as they really appear to be. What do we see when our eyes are closed? Do we see beauty? Do we see judgment? Do we see riches? Do we see poverty? Do we see people who are homeless and are filthy? Do we see different races and different cultures? Do we see people the way they really are? Do we see their size, the way they dress, etc? Believe it or not sometimes our open eyes blind us. We look with open eyes entirely different than with closed eyes.

The way we should start looking at people when our eyes are open is that everyone we see is a child of God. Maybe we need to close our eyes to see this so we don't see everything else about that person. Possibly we need to live with our eyes closed so we can see clearly. The clear vision is that EVERYONE is a child of God, No Exceptions, and should be treated and Seen as a child of God. God sees even the vilest sinner as a child of God and can call that person into a love relationship and so should we. He calls us to be part of His mission. We can see most clearly with our eyes closed. A great example of this was Samson. Samson looked at Delilah totally different with open eyes than he did when his eyes were burned out. It wasn't until the Philistines burned his eyes out that he could really see the real person that Delilah was. Read Judges Chapter 16.

Part 2 Listening With Our Eyes Closed

Do you know you also listen better when your eyes are closed? You can truly focus in on the Lord!!! You can hear from Him. Yes, God wants you to listen to Him, but he wants you to praise and worship Him also. You will be amazed how in tune you are with the Spirit when your eyes are closed. Be still and know that he is God. Proverbs 18:15 – The heart of the prudent acquires knowledge, And the ear of the wise seeks knowledge. Proverbs 17:27 – He who has knowledge spares his words, And a man of understanding is of a calm spirit. Proverbs 16:20 – He who heeds the word wisely will find good, And whoever trusts in the LORD, happy is he.

Samson always thought that his strength was in his hair, but he soon realized that his strength came from the Lord. Without his eyes he had to turn totally to God through prayer and forgiveness. He was now totally dependent on God and in tune with God.

Give it a try, you will be amazed at the results when you look and listen with your eyes closed. You will see clearly and hear things that you never imagined you could possibly hear. You will look at life entirely different and hopefully start looking and seeing the inward appearance of people and not the outward appearance. How beautiful you are with your eyes closed.

You have been chosen, are you ready? What are you waiting for? Question yourself and get out of spiritual and financial debt? What is church and why do you need the bible? How and why do you strengthen your belief? Are you in the age of fulfillment, what are you filling yourself up with? Is there retirement with God? What is your temple? Are revivals causing salvations today? What is important to you? What should you do after receiving salvation? Can you see good and evil? What do you see with your eyes closed and what do you hear with your eyes closed? Is it easy or hard to become a Christian and to live it out?

Easy—Hard

It is easy to become a Christian; it is hard to live it out. Or is it? (Mark 4:3-20) **3** "Listen! Behold, a sower went out to sow. **4** And it happened, as he sowed, that some seed fell by the wayside; and the birds of the air came and devoured it. **5** Some fell on stony ground, where it did not have much earth; and immediately it sprang up because it had no depth of earth. **6** But when the sun was up it was scorched, and because it had no root it withered away. **7** And some seed fell among thorns; and the thorns grew up and choked it, and it yielded no crop. **8** But other seed fell on good ground and yielded a crop that sprang up, increased and produced: some thirtyfold, some sixty, and some a hundred." **9** And He said to them, "He who has ears to hear, let him hear!" **10** But when He was alone, those around Him with the twelve asked Him about the parable. **11** And He said to them, "To you it has been given to know the mystery of the kingdom of God; but to those who are outside, all things come in parables, **12** so that' Seeing they may see and not perceive, And hearing they may hear and not understand; Lest they should turn, And their sins be forgiven them." **13** And He said to them, "Do you not understand this parable? How then will you understand all the parables? **14** The sower sows the word. **15** And these are the ones by the wayside where the word is sown. When they hear, Satan comes immediately and takes away the word that was sown in their hearts. **16** These likewise are the ones sown on stony ground who, when they hear the word, immediately receive it with gladness; **17** and they have no root in themselves, and so endure only for a time. Afterward, when tribulation or persecution arises for the word's sake, immediately they stumble. **18** Now these are the ones sown among thorns; they are the ones who hear the word, **19** and the cares of this world, the deceitfulness of riches, and the desires for other things entering in choke the word, and becomes unfruitful. **20** But these are the ones sown on good ground, those who hear the word, accept it, and bear fruit: some thirtyfold, some sixty, and some a hundred."

Easy: (A) Romans 10:9-10 and (B) II Corinthians 5:17 (A) **9** that if you confess with your mouth the Lord Jesus and believe in your heart that God has raised Him from the dead, you will be saved. **10** For with the heart one believes unto righteousness, and with the mouth confession is made unto salvation. (B) **17** Therefore, if anyone is in Christ, he is a new creation; old things have passed away; behold, all things have become new.

Hard: In John 16:33, Jesus tells us-In this world you will have trouble, but be of good cheer, I have overcome the world. (John 16:33) These things I have spoken to you, that in Me you may have peace. In the world you will have tribulation; but be of good cheer, I have overcome the world. In I Corinthians 10:13 the Word tells us No temptation has seized you except what is common to man. (I Corinthians 10:13) No temptation has overtaken you except such as is common to man; but God is faithful, who will not allow you to be tempted beyond what you are able, but with the temptation will also make the way of escape, that you may be able to bear it. In I Peter 5:8 it says The devil prowls around like a roaring lion looking for someone to devour. He is your enemy. (I Peter 5:8) Be sober, be vigilant; because your adversary the devil walks about like a roaring lion, seeking whom he may devour. Below are more scriptures you decide "Easy" or "Hard".

(James 1:19-25) **19** So then my beloved brethren, let every man be swift to hear, slow to speak, slow to wrath; **20** for the wrath of man does not produce the righteousness of God. **21** Therefore lay aside all filthiness and overflow of wickedness, and receive with meekness the implanted word, which is able to save your souls. **22** But be doers of the word, and not hearers only, deceiving yourselves. **23** For if anyone is a hearer of the word and not a doer, he is like a man observing his natural face in a mirror; **24** for he observes himself, goes away, and immediately forgets what kind of man he was. **25** But he who looks into the perfect law of liberty and continues in it, and is not a forgetful hearer but a doer of the work, this one will be blessed in what he does. (I John 1:9) If we confess our sins, He is faithful and just to forgive us our sins and to cleanse us from all unrighteousness. (Acts 2:38-39) **38** Then Peter said to them, "Repent, and let every one of you be baptized in the name of Jesus Christ for the remission of sins; and you shall receive the gift of the Holy Spirit. **39** For the promise is to you and to your children, and to all who are afar off, as many as the Lord our God will call." (I John 2:15-17) **15** Do not love the world or the things in the world. If anyone loves the world, the love of the Father is not in him. **16** For all that is in the world—the lust of the flesh, the lust of the eyes, and the pride of life—is not of the Father but is of the world. **17** And the world is passing away, and the lust of it; but he who does the will of God abides forever. (I John 4:4) You are of God, little children, and have overcome them, because He who is in you is greater than he who is in the world. (James 1:2-4 Trials and Temptations) **2** My brethren, count it all joy when you fall into various trials, **3** knowing that the testing of your faith produces patience. **4** But let patience have its perfect work, that you may be perfect and complete, lacking nothing. (Philippians 4:13) I can do all things through Christ who strengthens me. (Psalms 119:11) Your word I have hidden in my heart, That I might not sin against You. (James 1:14-15) **14** But each one is tempted when he is drawn away by his own desires and enticed. **15** Then, when desire has conceived, it gives birth to sin; and sin, when it is full-grown, brings forth death. (James 4:7-8) **7** Therefore submit to God. Resist the devil and he will flee from you. **8** Draw near to God and He will draw near to you. (Matthew 26:41) Watch and pray, lest you enter into temptation. The spirit indeed is willing, but the flesh is weak. (Matthew 4:4-11 What did Jesus do when he was tempted?) **4** But He answered and said, "It is written, 'Man shall not live by bread alone, but by every word that proceeds from the mouth of God." **5** Then the devil took Him up into the holy city, set Him on the pinnacle of the temple, **6** and said to Him, "If You are the Son of God, throw Yourself down. For it is written: 'He shall give His angels charge over you,' and, 'In their hands they shall bear you up, Lest you dash your foot against a stone." **7** Jesus said to him, "It is written again, 'You shall not tempt the LORD your God." **8** Again, the devil took Him up on an exceedingly high mountain, and showed Him all the kingdoms of the world and their glory. **9** And he said to Him, "All these things I will give You if You will fall down and worship me." **10** Then Jesus said to him, "Away with you, Satan! For it is written, 'You shall worship the LORD your God, and Him only you shall serve." **11** Then the devil left Him, and behold, angels came and ministered to Him. (Ephesians 6:10-20) **10** Finally, my brethren, be strong in the Lord and in the power of His might. **11** Put on the whole armor of God, that you may be able to stand against the wiles of the devil. **12** For we do not wrestle against flesh and blood, but against principalities, against powers, against the rulers of the darkness of this age, against spiritual hosts of wickedness in the heavenly places. **13** Therefore take up the whole armor of God, that you may be able to with-stand in the evil day, and having done all, to stand. **14** Stand therefore, having girded your waist with truth, having put on the breastplate of righteousness, **15** and having shod your

The Best Investment Money Can't Buy

feet with the preparation of the gospel of peace; **16** above all, taking the shield of faith with which you will be able to quench all the fiery darts of the wicked one. **17** And take the helmet of salvation, and the sword of the Spirit, which is the word of God; **18** praying always with all prayer and supplication in the Spirit, being watchful to this end with all perseverance and supplication for all the saints— **19** and for me, that utterance may be given to me, that I may open my mouth boldly to make known the mystery of the gospel, **20** for which I am an ambassador in chains; that in it I may speak boldly, as I ought to speak. (II Corinthians 10:4-6) **4** For the weapons of our warfare are not carnal but mighty in God for pulling down strongholds, **5** casting down arguments and every high thing that exalts itself against the knowledge of God, bringing every thought into captivity to the obedience of Christ, **6** and being ready to punish all disobedience when your obedience is fulfilled. Remember Mark 4:3-20? Which one is you? "Easy" or "Hard" let's break it down: Verse 15 – Hear the Word and is then taken away by Satan. Verse 16-17 – Hear the Word, receive it, have no root, and only last a short time. Verse 18-19 – Hear the Word, it is chocked out and is unfruitful. Verse 20 – Hear the Word, accept it and produce a crop. You can get to verse 20 it is your choice!

You have been chosen, are you ready? What are you waiting for? Question yourself and get out of spiritual and financial debt? What is church and why do you need the bible? How and why do you strengthen your belief? Are you in the age of fulfillment, what are you filling yourself up with? Is there retirement with God? What is your temple? Are revivals causing salvations today? What is important to you? What should you do after receiving salvation? Can you see good and evil? What do you see with your eyes closed and what do you hear with your eyes closed? Is it easy or hard to become a Christian and to live it out? Is there good news or bad news with Christ?

Good News—Bad News

Have you ever heard the saying, do you want to hear the good news or the bad news first?

(I John 5:11-12) gives us the good news and bad news about life. **11** And this is the testimony: that God has given us eternal life, and this life is in His Son. **12** He who has the Son has life; he who does not have the Son of God does not have life. (Acts 3:23) And it shall be that every soul who will not hear that Prophet shall be utterly destroyed from among the people. (II Timothy 3 **Perilous Times and Perilous Men**) **1** But know this, that in the last days perilous times will come: **2** For men will be lovers of themselves, lovers of money, boasters, proud, blasphemers, disobedient to parents, unthankful, unholy, **3** unloving, unforgiving, slanderers, without self-control, brutal, despisers of good, **4** traitors, headstrong, haughty, lovers of pleasure rather than lovers of God, **5** having a form of godliness but denying its power. And from such people turn away! **6** For of this sort are those who creep into households and make captives of gullible women loaded down with sins, led away by various lusts, **7** always learning and never able to come to the knowledge of the truth. **8** Now as Jannes and Jambres resisted Moses, so do these also resist the truth: men of corrupt minds, disapproved concerning the faith; **9** but they will progress no further, for their folly will be manifest to all, as theirs also was. (**The Man of God and the Word of God**) **10** But you have carefully followed my doctrine, manner of life, purpose, faith, longsuffering, love, perseverance, **11** persecutions, afflictions, which happened to me at Antioch, at Iconium, at Lystra—what persecutions I endured. And out of them all the Lord delivered me. **12** Yes, and all who desire to live godly in Christ Jesus will suffer persecution. **13** But evil men and impostors will grow worse and worse, deceiving and being deceived. **14** But you must continue in the things which you have learned and been assured of, knowing from whom you have learned them, **15** and that from childhood you have known the Holy Scriptures, which are able to make you wise for salvation through faith which is in Christ Jesus. **16** All Scripture is given by inspiration of God, and is profitable for doctrine, for reproof, for correction, for instruction in righteousness, **17** that the man of God may be complete, thoroughly equipped for every good work.

(Jude) **1** Jude, a bondservant of Jesus Christ, and brother of James, To those who are called, sanctified by God the Father, and preserved in Jesus Christ: **2** Mercy, peace, and love be multiplied to you. **3** Beloved, while I was very diligent to write to you concerning our common salvation, I found it necessary to write to you exhorting you to contend earnestly for the faith which was once for all delivered to the saints. **4** For certain men have crept in unnoticed, who long ago were marked out for this condemnation, ungodly men, who turn the grace of our God into lewdness and deny the only Lord God and our Lord Jesus Christ. **5** But I want to remind you, though you once knew this, that the Lord, having saved the people out of the land of Egypt, afterward destroyed those who did not believe. **6** And the angels who did not keep their proper domain, but left their own abode, He has reserved in everlasting chains under darkness for the judgment of the great day; **7** as Sodom and Gomorrah, and the cities around them in a similar manner to these, having given themselves over to sexual immorality and gone after strange flesh, are set forth as an example, suffering the vengeance of eternal fire. **8** Likewise also these dreamers defile the flesh, reject authority, and speak evil of dignitaries. **9** Yet Michael the archangel, in contending with the devil, when he disputed about the body of Moses, dared not bring against him a reviling accusation, but said, "The Lord rebuke you!" **10** But these speak evil of whatever they do not know; and whatever they know naturally, like brute beasts, in these things they corrupt themselves. **11** Woe to them! For they have gone in the way of Cain, have run greedily in the error of Balaam for profit, and perished in the rebellion of Korah. **12** These are spots in your love feasts, while they feast with you without fear, serving only themselves. They are clouds without water, carried about by the winds; late autumn trees without fruit, twice dead, pulled up by the roots; **13** raging waves of the sea, foaming up their own shame; wandering stars for whom is reserved the blackness of darkness forever. **14** Now Enoch, the seventh from Adam, prophesied about these men also, saying, "Behold, the Lord comes with ten thousands of His saints, **15** to execute judgment on all, to convict all who are ungodly among them of all their ungodly deeds which they have committed in an ungodly way, and of all the harsh things which ungodly sinners have spoken against Him." **16** These are grumblers, complainers, walking according to their own lusts; and they mouth great swelling words, flattering people to gain advantage. **17** But you, beloved, remember the words which were spoken before by the apostles of our Lord Jesus Christ: **18** how they told you that there would be mockers in the last time who would walk according to their own ungodly lusts. **19** These are sensual persons, who cause divisions, not having the Spirit. **20** But you, beloved, building yourselves up on your most holy faith, praying in the Holy Spirit, **21** keep yourselves in the love of God, looking for the mercy of our Lord Jesus Christ unto eternal life. **22** And on some have compassion, making a distinction; **23** but others save with fear, pulling them out of the fire, hating even the garment defiled by the flesh. **24** Now to Him who is able to keep you from stumbling, And to present you faultless Before the presence of His glory with exceeding joy, **25** To God our Savior, Who alone is wise, Be glory and majesty, Dominion and power, Both now and forever. Amen.

The final good news (Revelation 22:12-14) **12** "And behold, I am coming quickly, and My reward is with Me, to give to every one according to his work. **13** I am the Alpha and the Omega, the Beginning and the End, the First and the Last." **14** Blessed are those who do His commandments, that they may have the right to the tree of life, and may enter through the gates into the city.

You have been chosen, are you ready? What are you waiting for? Question yourself and get out of spiritual and financial debt? What is church and why do you need the bible? How and why do you strengthen your belief? Are you in the age of fulfillment, what are you filling yourself up with? Is there retirement with God? What is your temple? Are revivals causing salvations today? What is important to you? What should you do after receiving salvation? Can you see good and evil? What do you see with your eyes closed and what do you hear with your eyes closed? Is it easy or hard to become a Christian and to live it out? Is there good news or bad news with Christ? Are we like trees?

We Are Like Trees

W e are like the trees that God created, he planted the 1st seed and it was planted correctly with a firm foundation. We as humans are the same as the trees, he planted the 1st seed and if we plant our foundation firmly in this seed we will prosper. If we don't plant our seed in the proper soil, we just like the tree will not grow. We are like the trees; we need dirt, water, and fertilizer. The dirt is the foundation or Jesus. The water makes us grow or the Word. The fertilizer enhances the growth or fellowship with other believers, the fertilizer leads us and guides us or the Holy Spirit. We need to be rooted with a solid foundation or Jesus, watered with God's Word, and fertilized with the Holy Spirit, through prayer, fasting, and fellowship with other believers.

You can be planted in good dirt just like a tree, but if you are not watered and fertilized, you just like the tree will die. How often does a tree need these things to grow? We are like the trees.

You have been chosen, are you ready? What are you waiting for? Question yourself and get out of spiritual and financial debt? What is church and why do you need the bible? How and why do you strengthen your belief? Are you in the age of fulfillment, what are you filling yourself up with? Is there retirement with God? What is your temple? Are revivals causing salvations today? What is important to you? What should you do after receiving salvation? Can you see good and evil? What do you see with your eyes closed and what do you hear with your eyes closed? Is it easy or hard to become a Christian and to live it out? Is there good news or bad news with Christ? Are we like trees? How do you weather the storm?

Weather The Storm

We weather the storm by having each other and sharing our gifts to help each other out of any and all situations. These gifts come from the father and are only possible to have because of Christ. These gifts are to be used for the edifying of the saints.

Sometimes it takes a storm to get our attention, to call on others to help us through our situations and to call on Jesus for all our needs. We should put Him first and our brothers and sisters second. We should depend on each other, fellowship with each other, and share the Word with each other. We get focused on the eye of the storm instead of keeping our focus on the eye of creation, the eye of control, the eye of everything. The center of the storm should be Christ. Think about it, in times of trouble how should we be reacting and responding to the storm? Sometimes it takes a storm for God to get our attention. This is a growth opportunity to show our true colors, our faith, our love, our servant-hood, and our calling.

We weather the storm by having each other, sharing our gifts, prayer, fasting, fellowship, praise and worship, and keeping our focus on the eye of creation. What is your storm today?

You have been chosen, are you ready? What are you waiting for? Question yourself and get out of spiritual and financial debt? What is church and why do you need the bible? How and why do you strengthen your belief? Are you in the age of fulfillment, what are you filling yourself up with? Is there retirement with God? What is your temple? Are revivals causing salvations today? What is important to you? What should you do after receiving salvation? Can you see good and evil? What do you see with your eyes closed and what do you hear with your eyes closed? Is it easy or hard to become a Christian and to live it out? Is there good news or bad news with Christ? Are we like trees? How do you weather the storm? Are you unemployed and out work?

Unemployed And Out Of Work

Are you out of work and want to join a business where you will never be out of work again and have the best benefits you can ever imagine? If you answered yes then it is time to join the business of saving mankind. Let's look at the parts of this business. At the top we have Father, Son, and Holy Spirit or the trinity. God the Father is the manager and enabler. God the Son is the assistant manager who makes salvation available and intercedes for us to the Father. God the Holy Spirit is the communicator or public relations manager who speaks to us and comforts us and also speaks to the Father when we do not know what to say.

This business needs a lot of employees, who do you think that could be? Yes, God's children. You were created in the image of God with Spirit, Soul, and Body. The Spirit allows us to receive and transmit spiritual messages. The Soul is the eternal essence of a person, created to self-manage all aspects of the person. The Body is the temple for your Spirit and Soul. What is our job in this everlasting business? Our job is to be servants of Christ and to do His work by sharing the Mystery of Christ and telling the good news to others.

What do you need to have to accomplish the good works that God has prepared beforehand? Yes, God predestined you even before you were born to do His work, see you were really never unemployed unless you have stopped doing the Fathers work that he had called you to do. He has equipped you with three very important things to accomplish His work: Faith, Hope, and Love. Faith is simply to believe in God; Hope is to trust in an outcome, eternity; and Love means you are devoted to God and your brothers and sisters. Faith, Hope, and Love are a trinity in itself if you think about it. Without faith you can't please God and without faith you do not have Hope. Faith multiplied by Love equals the spiritual power of Hope developed in the souls of those who have received the gospel. You have the best equipment that money can't buy; you have a power source to be able to do your work "God", you have an intercessor/savior to help you through your rough work days "Christ", and you have an unending link to talk to the managers and be comforted "The Holy Spirit".

If you get employment at this business you will never be out of work again if you do what the manual tells you to do which is the Bible. Oh, the benefits. God will supply ALL of your needs while on earth and he will have streets of gold ready for you when you retire, meaning go to heaven. You will not have any sickness anymore, you will be in his choir singing praises, and these are a few of the wonderful things of this business. Are you employed yet or still unemployed and out of work?

You have been chosen, are you ready? What are you waiting for? Question yourself and get out of spiritual and financial debt? What is church and why do you need the bible? How and why do you strengthen your belief? Are you in the age of fulfillment, what are you filling yourself up with? Is there retirement with God? What is your temple? Are revivals causing salvations today? What is important to you? What should you do after receiving salvation? Can you see good and evil? What do you see with your eyes closed and what do you hear with your eyes closed? Is it easy or hard to become a Christian and to live it out? Is there good news or bad news with Christ? Are we like trees? How do you weather the storm? Are you unemployed and out work? Are you having a pity party?

Pity Party

It is easy to thank God when he does what we want, but God does not always do what we want. Read the book of Job. God doesn't owe anyone anything, not any reasons, not any explanations, nothing because God is God. He knows what he is doing. When you can't understand his ways, trust his heart, but don't have a pity party.

If you love God he knows you. Think before you speak, and be careful about what you say to God. God is in heaven the holy place. If you chase the things of the world, you will end up with sadness, anger, sorrow, sickness, and defeat; you will end up having a pity party.

When God made people he made them good, but they have found all kinds of ways to be bad and then blame someone else for their problems! Don't leave your job just because your boss is angry with you or you are angry at your boss. You can always find reasons and make excuses why you should or should not do something. Remember anger is one letter short of danger. Proverbs says to remain calm and you will solve great problems. If you give up when trouble comes, it shows that you are weak and you will be having another pity party.

Read about the Israelites when God used Moses to set them free from Pharaoh. How and why did they continue to have pity parties? Read about the Israelites when they came back to Judah after being in Exile and were suppose to rebuild the temple. Read about Jonah when God asked him to go preach at Nineveh. Read about Hagar when Sarai kicked her out and sent her away. Read about David when King Saul was chasing after him to kill him. Read about Peter when he denied he knew Christ.

Life is always about choices; you can choose to be happy or sad, motivated or unmotivated, or choose to have a pity party or not have a pity party. One thing is for sure in life, you will have trials and tribulations and you can choose to have a pity party or respond in a Godly manner and be joyous.

You have been chosen, are you ready? What are you waiting for? Question yourself and get out of spiritual and financial debt? What is church and why do you need the bible? How and why do you strengthen your belief? Are you in the age of fulfillment, what are you filling yourself up with? Is there retirement with God? What is your temple? Are revivals causing salvations today? What is important to you? What should you do after receiving salvation? Can you see good and evil? What do you see with your eyes closed and what do you hear with your eyes closed? Is it easy or hard to become a Christian and to live it out? Is there good news or bad news with Christ? Are we like trees? How do you weather the storm? Are you unemployed and out work? Are you having a pity party? Are you the right person for the job?

The Right Person For The Job!

G od always has the right person for the job. The right person for the job might argue and even disagree with God and possibly will not even do the job God has called him/her to do, but more than likely they will end up doing the job. Why, because they are the right person for the job and have been called by God to do the job.

The bible has endless examples of people called by God to do his work; they were the right person for the job. The major people called by God to do his work were Noah, Abram later called Abraham, Sarai later called Sarah, Isaac, Eliezer, Rebekah, Jacob/Israel, Joseph, Moses, Aaron, Joshua the son of Nun, Caleb the son of Jephunneh, Deborah, Gideon, Samson, Naomi, Samuel, Saul, David, Nathan, Solomon,

Elijah, Elisha, Job, Daniel, Esther, Ezra, Nehemiah, the Prophets, Zacharias and Elizabeth, Mary and Joseph, John the Baptist, JESUS, the disciples, Saul named Paul, many others in the Bible and YOU!

Jonah is probably the best example of someone called to do God's work that was the right person for the job, but disagreed with God. God had ordered Jonah to go to Nineveh to minister to them, but Jonah despised them and did not want to minister to them so Jonah tries to avoid God's calling by going to Joppa and sailing to Tarshish. While on the boat a huge storm evolves and this is not any ordinary storm, this storm was happening for a reason. The sailors realized that something out of the ordinary was happening and cast lots and learned that Jonah was to blame. Jonah admits he is the reason for this unordinary storm and tells them to throw him overboard and the storm will subside. The sailors did not want to throw Jonah overboard so they tried to get to shore and drop off Jonah, but could not so they throw him overboard and the storm stops. God has called Jonah to do a job so he is miraculously saved by being swallowed by a big fish. Jonah now has time to think about his choice.

While in the big fish, Jonah prays and asks God for forgiveness and God commands the big fish to vomit Jonah out. God again tells Jonah to go minister to the people of Nineveh and Jonah obeys this time. He is the right person for the job. The people of Nineveh heed Jonah's message and warning so God spared them. What happened to Jonah and what was his response? As Paul Harvey would say, "you need to read the rest of the story".

We may be called to do things we do not want to do, but that doesn't mean we aren't the right person for the job. Keep this in mind when you are asked to do something you may not necessarily want to do as in the case of Jonah. When God calls you, you are the right person for the job.

You have been chosen, are you ready? What are you waiting for? Question yourself and get out of spiritual and financial debt? What is church and why do you need the bible? How and why do you strengthen your belief? Are you in the age of fulfillment, what are you filling yourself up with? Is there retirement with God? What is your temple? Are revivals causing salvations today? What is important to you? What should you do after receiving salvation? Can you see good and evil? What do you see with your eyes closed and what do you hear with your eyes closed? Is it easy or hard to become a Christian and to live it out? Is there good news or bad news with Christ? Are we like trees? How do you weather the storm? Are you unemployed and out work? Are you having a pity party? Are you the right person for the job? What is your calling?

Get Excited About Your Calling

You have been called by God to be someone that is important to someone else. When you were young and you received that special phone call, didn't you get excited?

- Why did you get excited? You got excited because that phone call was important to you. Your phone call is important to someone else out in the world also.
- You got excited because someone had something that you wanted to hear. Your call is important for someone to hear what you have to say and what they want to hear.

- You got excited because the phone call was refreshing. Your call can be refreshing to someone else.

Many have been called, but few are chosen. Why, possibly they aren't answering the call. If you do not answer the call you do not know what the message is! You will not be able to share that message with others.

Who has been called? You all have been called. Please, please answer the call, get excited about the call. Your call is important for someone else. Ephesians 4 says, Christians are called to live for Christ and walk even as He walked, it is a high calling. You need to walk worthy of the calling with which you were called. You should walk with lowliness, gentleness, longsuffering, bearing with one another in love.

It is time to get excited about your call. Your call is important for your church, your family, your neighbor, your county, your state, your nation, and for the world. Answer the call!

You have been chosen, are you ready? What are you waiting for? Question yourself and get out of spiritual and financial debt? What is church and why do you need the bible? How and why do you strengthen your belief? Are you in the age of fulfillment, what are you filling yourself up with? Is there retirement with God? What is your temple? Are revivals causing salvations today? What is important to you? What should you do after receiving salvation? Can you see good and evil? What do you see with your eyes closed and what do you hear with your eyes closed? Is it easy or hard to become a Christian and to live it out? Is there good news or bad news with Christ? Are we like trees? How do you weather the storm? Are you unemployed and out work? Are you having a pity party? Are you the right person for the job? What is your calling? How do you honor God?

Conclusion: Honor God

(Ecclesiastes 12:9-14 "Scriptures quoted from The Holy Bible, New Century Version, copyright © 2005 by Thomas Nelson, Inc. Used by permission."). **9** The Teacher was very wise and taught the people what he knew. He very carefully thought about, studied, and set in order many wise teachings. **10** The Teacher looked for just the right words to write what is dependable and true.

11 Words from wise people are like sharp sticks used to guide animals. They are like nails that have been driven in firmly. Altogether they are wise teachings that come from one Shepherd. **12** So be careful, my son, about other teachings. People are always writing books, and too much study will make you tired.

13 Now, everything has been heard,

so I give my final advice:

Honor God and obey his commands,

because this is all people must do.

14 God will judge everything,

even what is done in secret,

the good and the evil.

You have been chosen, are you ready? What are you waiting for? Question yourself and get out of spiritual and financial debt? What is church and why do you need the bible? How and why do you strengthen your belief? Are you in the age of fulfillment, what are you filling yourself up with? Is there retirement with God? What is your temple? Are revivals causing salvations today? What is important to you? What should you do after receiving salvation? Can you see good and evil? What do you see with your eyes closed and what do you hear with your eyes closed? Is it easy or hard to become a Christian and to live it out? Is there good news or bad news with Christ? Are we like trees? How do you weather the storm? Are you unemployed and out work?

Are you having a pity party? Are you the right person for the

job? What is your calling? How do you honor God? Are you

ready to spread these messages and be a blessing to others?

Summary and Biography

These messages were written from ideas that God gave me from a variety of settings. Some messages came from ideas I heard during church sermons, Christian broadcasting, crusades, reading books, events that have happened, my own personal experiences, the Bible, and a mission trip to Africa.

Key words or phrases would be said or read about during these different settings and then God would inspire me to write about what was heard or read. Some ideas came from personal experiences and then confirmed by other messages that were being preached. I write down almost every message that I hear preached at Church, or at the Crusades.

The final inspiration to write this book came from my circumstances at church. I had a lot of messages ready to preach, but was not having an opportunity to preach them. I was starting to get bitter and God inspired me to put these messages in a book and said the messages would reach a lot more people this way. I heard the call and did what God called me to do and now I am better not bitter.

I have been a Christian since I was thirteen and a practicing Christian since I was twenty four. Duties in the Church have included: singing in the Choir, leading praise and worship, teaching Junior High and Adult Sunday School, Lay Leader Committee, Finance Committee, Superintendent of Adult Sunday School, Education Chair, Certified Lay Speaker, and Youth Counselor. God has called me to teach, preach, go on a mission trip to Africa, and now write this book. Please help get these messages out to the world. May God richly bless you!

Sincerely,

Eric England

Endnotes

[1]Holy Bible New Living Translation copyright © 1996, 2004 by Tyndale Charitable Trust. Used by permission of Tyndale House Publishers.

[2]Tim Rose, Evangelist, Hollister, Missouri Crusade 2006.

[3]Henry T. Blackaby and Claude V. King, The Experiencing God Bible (pp 1847-1850), Copyright © 1994 by Broadman & Holman Publishers.

[4]Henry T. Blackaby and Claude V. King, The Experiencing God Bible (pp 1847-1850), Copyright © 1994 by Broadman & Holman Publishers.

[5]Henry T. Blackaby and Claude V. King, The Experiencing God Bible (pp 1847-1850), Copyright © 1994 by Broadman & Holman Publishers.

[6]Henry T. Blackaby and Claude V. King, The Experiencing God Bible (pp1847-1850), Copyright © 1994 by Broadman & Holman Publishers.

[7]R.A. Torrey The New Topical Textbook, published 1897, www.bible-topics.com copyright 2007 Brandon Staggs.

[8]R.A. Torrey The New Topical Textbook, published 1897, www.bible-topics.com copyright 2007 Brandon Staggs.

[9]R.A. Torrey The New Topical Textbook, published 1897, www.bible-topics.com copyright 2007 Brandon Staggs.

[10]R.A. Torrey The New Topical Textbook, published 1897, www.bible-topics.com copyright 2007 Brandon Staggs.

[11]R.A. Torrey The New Topical Textbook, published 1897, www.bible-topics.com copyright 2007 Brandon Staggs.

[12]The American Heritage School Dictionary, © 1972 by American Heritage Publishing Co., Inc.

[13]The American Heritage School Dictionary, © 1972 by American Heritage Publishing Co., Inc.

[14]Marilyn Adamson Is There a God? www.everystudent. com/features/isthere.html.

[15]Marilyn Adamson Is There a God? www.everystudent.com/features/isthere.html.

[16]Christian Apologetics & Research Ministry

© Matthew J. Slick, 1995-2009, www.carm.org/christianity/bible/prophecy-bible-and-jesus.

Breinigsville, PA USA
18 February 2010
232739BV00001B/4/P